MAKING THE CHANGE

DISCOVERING GOD'S AMAZING GENEROSITY

Studies for Individuals and Small Groups

Making the Change

Copyright @2017

All rights reserved.

Published by Generous Heart.

Unless otherwise noted, Scripture quotations are from the Holy Bible:

New International Version – UK, Copyright © 1973, 1978, 1984 by the International Bible Society.

ISBN: 978-1-9997292-2-6

Printed in the United Kingdom

Cover design and interior layout by: Loulita Gill Design

Do you have a smartphone?

Download a FREE Barcode Scanner APP which will allow you to go straight to the website to view our videos

You can check out all the videos in Making the Change by going to the website or using the Barcode Scanner below.

www.generousheart.co.uk/videos

www.yourmoneycounts.org.uk/video

CONTENTS

5 **INTRODUCTION**
   The Challenge
   The Course
   The Bible
   Pause for Thought
   Group Sessions

13 **SESSION 1**
   "Less is More"
   A Blueprint for Living

21 **GROUP SESSION**

25 **SESSION 2**
   "Stress is Bad"
   Free to Serve Him

31 **GROUP SESSION**

37	**SESSION 3**	
	"Giving is Good"	
	Growing in Generosity	
45	**GROUP SESSION**	

49	**SESSION 4**	
	"Tomorrow Matters"	
	Changing how you Live Today	
55	**GROUP SESSION**	

61	**CONCLUSION**	
64	Appendix 1	Full List of Videos
66	Appendix 2	Video Information with Questions
70	Appendix 3	Other Books

INTRODUCTION

THE CHALLENGE
"Discovering Generosity"

Over the next few weeks, we will be facing the challenge of how we can learn to give more generously. But if we want to 'Discover God's Amazing Generosity', we must start by making an honest evaluation of our current attitude towards our possessions.

Money is a pressing issue for most people. A great many of us spend a huge amount of time making money, spending money, worrying about money, fighting over money or simply trying to protect our money. And, of course, we dare not ignore the alarming statistics that tell a story of rapidly increasing consumer debt, saving rates that have 'fallen off of a cliff' and conflicts over money that are the cause of so much unhappiness and discontent.

It need not be like this. Money and possessions can have a 'cancerous effect' on our lives, but it is possible to embrace a far healthier lifestyle. We can make changes; changes that will radically transform our lives for the better. This will inevitably mean cultivating a generous spirit.

Many of us avoid discussing money issues, but it is important to realise that talking can prove very helpful. More than that, planning can become the key to financial freedom.

'Making the Change' will help you discover a new set of priorities – priorities that will set you free to become generous, both now and in the future. In so doing, you will experience the abundant life Jesus promised His disciples.

INTRODUCTION

You have already taken the first step to achieving this, whether you're trying to get out of debt or simply wanting to devise a plan for the future. This is a wonderful opportunity for you to lay a foundation that will last a lifetime. We can all invest in a brighter tomorrow by 'Making the Change' today. But be aware of this: our relationship to money inevitably involves our relationship with God, because in the final analysis it reveals the things we value most.

Let's face it. We are all innately materialistic. We instinctively want more and more. And there is only one antidote to materialism: generosity. Every act of generosity is a spiritual victory and will help us become more like the God we see revealed in Jesus. For He is nothing if not infinitely generous, and He expects us to reflect His image in the way we live and behave.

It is our prayer that these times together will prove to be times of transformation, a transformation that will inspire us to worship the God who has given us everything we possess.

THE COURSE
"Making the Change"

This course has been shaped by the recognition that Christians acknowledge Jesus as 'Lord'. In other words, we recognise that everything we possess ultimately belongs to Him and that we will have to give an account of what we've done on the day we meet Him, because meet Him we certainly will.

In essence, 'Making the Change' consists of four interactive sessions, each of which will offer you an opportunity to explore and discuss a range of video and biblical material. Each session has a separate introduction that needs to be studied in order for you to get the most out of this course. You will also find it helpful to review the notes and revisit the videos and biblical passages following your time together. This will allow you to discover what God is trying to say to you.

SESSION 1

"Less is More"
A Blueprint for Living

SESSION 2

"Stress is Bad"
Free to Serve Him

SESSION 3

"Giving is Good"
Growing in Generosity

SESSION 4

"Tomorrow Matters"
Changing how you Live Today

THE BIBLE
"Wisdom from Above"

These studies have been written from the conviction that life 'can only get better' when we allow the Bible to shape our lives since it tells us what our Creator wants us to know. The Apostle Paul operated on this understanding, as we can see from this piece of advice he offered his friend Timothy:

All Scripture is God-breathed and is useful for teaching, rebuking, correcting and training in righteousness, so that the servant of God may be thoroughly equipped for every good work. 2 Timothy 3:16-17.

And so, right at the outset, it is worth underlining several key truths.

Firstly, in considering our attitude towards our possessions, we are dealing with a very important subject. In fact, the Bible contains more verses dealing with this issue than any other subject, apart from God Himself. More than fifteen percent of Jesus' recorded words deal with this subject, and more than half of His parables revolve around the handling of money and possessions. To help you appreciate this, we have produced a free book entitled, 'Foundation Truth on Money and Possessions', which can be downloaded from the website.

Download your free copy of 'Foundation Truth on Money and Possessions' from: **www.yourmoneycounts.org.uk**

Secondly, as you read the scriptures it will soon become clear that 'God's economy' is very different to ours, and that this will inevitably bring challenges given the fact that our approach has been shaped by human values and priorities. Therefore, it is important that we ask ourselves how our faith should impact the way we handle our money, not least because the Bible warns us of the consequences that will follow if we don't manage our possessions in the way God expects us.

INTRODUCTION

Thirdly, by its very nature, the Bible is not written topic by topic. The various passages were written at different times and in very different contexts. When they are viewed as a totality, however, it is obvious that the biblical authors operated on the understanding that (a) 'man's economy' has some very serious fault lines, and (b) 'God's economy' can never fail.

Fourthly, we need to be aware of the fact that we are constantly making decisions about the way we handle our possessions. In fact, we probably think about money at some point every day. And it's worth recognising that those we count as rich face just as many challenges as those we consider as poor.

Given this, we must come to terms with the fact that the way we use our possessions reveals our true priorities, not least how important the Lord is to us. Jesus understood this and was keen to stress that our hearts will follow the things we treasure and desire.

"No one can serve two masters. Either you will hate the one and love the other, or you will be devoted to the one and despise the other. You cannot serve both God and money."
Matthew 6:24.

Fifthly, we should allow the Bible to shape our attitudes and behaviour. By doing so, we will discover the freedom God wants us to enjoy. Indeed, viewing things from an eternal perspective can help us escape the gravitational pull of contemporary materialism.

And he told them this parable: "The ground of a certain rich man yielded an abundant harvest. He thought to himself, 'What shall I do? I have no place to store my crops.'

Then he said, 'This is what I'll do. I will tear down my barns and build bigger ones, and there I will store my surplus grain. And I'll say to myself, "You have plenty of grain laid up for many years. Take life easy; eat, drink and be merry."'

But God said to him, 'You fool! This very night your life will be demanded from you. Then who will get what you have prepared for yourself?'

This is how it will be with whoever stores up things for themselves but is not rich toward God."
Luke 12:16-21.

PAUSE FOR THOUGHT
"A Time to Reflect"

At this point in the session, you might find it helpful to spend some time reflecting on the meaning and the implications of the scripture verses given. Ask yourself what they tell you about your current values and attitude. Be honest, and ask God to give you the insights you need. In developing your love relationship with Jesus, it can help to ask questions, such as:

- What new things have I learned from these passages of scripture?
- Are there any clear instructions?
- Is He promising me anything?
- How should I apply them to the way I live at the moment?

Look for words of love and value. Pray simply and meaningfully. For example, you might want to say something like this: "Father God (Daddy). What do You want to chat about? As I sit silently in Your presence, what do You want to say to me? Please speak deeply into my heart."

Why not jot down one or two major themes and choose a verse that stands out from the rest? You could even make it your verse of the day. Actions like this can often help us hear from God.

And be prepared to share what you have learned from your individual study from the "laying Foundation Section" when you meet for your group session.

GROUP SESSIONS
"Opportunities for Making the Change"

Each of the four group sessions will include the following five sections:

1. Prayer

This is an opportunity to benefit from the wonderful assurance that we have a personal relationship with the God who created us and knows what is best for us. Jesus recognised the need to pray and we would do well to imitate Him.

His approach is summed up best in John chapter 5. Jesus was being criticised for 'breaking the rules' because He healed someone on the Sabbath. But this did not 'faze' Him. As far as He was concerned, He would do what His Father told Him to do (verses 19-20).

Why should we be any different given the fact that He has said: "As the Father has sent me, I am sending you."? (John 20:21).

In fact, Jesus emphasised the importance of prayer on many occasions. Here is but one example:

"So, I say to you: Ask and it will be given to you; seek and you will find; knock and the door will be opened to you. For everyone who asks receives; the one who seeks finds; and to the one who knocks, the door will be opened."
Luke 11:9-10.

"Ask and it will be given to you; seek and you will find; knock and the door will be opened to you. For everyone who asks receives; the one who seeks finds; and to the one who knocks, the door will be opened."
Matthew 7:7-8.

Let's be encouraged. Jesus tells us that if we ask (and the implication is that we keep on asking), our prayers will not go unrewarded. And if this were not enough, He makes the same point using two other images. We are to seek (and keep on seeking), because we will discover what we are looking for, and we are to carry on knocking at the door, because we will be allowed in.

These assurances can give us the confidence to ask God to be present in our sessions, affirming what we are doing right and correcting us when we need to change direction.

2. Teaching

You will either watch one of the videos and/or read a section of the Bible.

For the word of God is alive and active. Sharper than any double-edged sword, it penetrates even to dividing soul and spirit, joints and marrow; it judges the thoughts and attitudes of the heart. Nothing in all creation is hidden from God's sight. Everything is uncovered and laid bare before the eyes of him to whom we must give account.
Hebrews 4:12-13.

3. Application

You will be asked to respond to a set of questions that have been devised to clarify the principles underlying each session. There will be an opportunity to respond openly and honestly without fear of rejection or condemnation. The need for confidentiality will be stressed and there will be an opportunity to pray whenever the need arises. All this will be done in the confidence that we find in this next verse of scripture:

I keep asking that the God of our Lord Jesus Christ, the glorious Father, may give you the Spirit of wisdom and revelation, so that you may know him better. I pray that the eyes of your heart may be enlightened in order that you may know the hope to which he has called you, the riches of his glorious inheritance in his holy people, and his incomparably great power for us who believe.
Ephesians 1:17-19.

4. Transformation

This course is not intended to be purely academic. It is intended to be life-changing. Accordingly, you will be encouraged to think about what needs to be done before you meet for your next group session.

James, the brother of Jesus, has some timely words of wisdom here:

Anyone who listens to the word but does not do what it says is like someone who looks at his face in a mirror and, after looking at himself, goes away and immediately forgets what he looks like. But whoever looks intently into the perfect law that gives freedom, and continues in it—not forgetting what they have heard, but doing it—they will be blessed in what they do.
James 1:23-25.

5. Prayer

Every session will close with prayer. This will provide you with yet another opportunity to thank the Lord for what He has been doing among you, as well as ask Him for His help to remember and apply what He is guiding you to do.

Solomon can help us here. He wrote:

My son, do not forget my teaching, but keep my commands in your heart, for they will prolong your life many years and bring you peace and prosperity.

Let love and faithfulness never leave you; bind them around your neck, write them on the tablet of your heart. Then you will win favour and a good name in the sight of God and man.

Trust in the Lord with all your heart and lean not on your own understanding; in all your ways submit to him, and he will make your paths straight.

INTRODUCTION

Do not be wise in your own eyes; fear the Lord and shun evil. This will bring health to your body and nourishment to your bones.

Honour the Lord with your wealth, with the first fruits of all your crops; then your barns will be filled to overflowing, and your vats will brim over with new wine.
Proverbs 3:1-10.

PREPARATION
LAYING FOUNDATIONS

These preparatory studies will serve as an introduction to help you prepare for your interactive group sessions. The preparation laying foundation sessions will be best completed in two to three individual 30 minute in the week prior to the group session

SESSION 1

"LESS IS MORE" | A Blueprint for Living

KEY MEMORY VERSE

Better one handful with tranquility than two handfuls with toil and chasing after the wind.
Ecclesiastes 4:6.

INTRODUCTION

Watch Video 2
God Owns Everything – Less is More

Where we unpack and discuss biblical teaching points for you to consider the challenge set forth as well as take part in a discussion relating to the subject. As always, these opinions are no substitute for examining the Word of God. Also, where appropriate, review the video with the worksheet. The video and worksheet can be found on the website.

2 Timothy 3:16-17, NLT tells us: *All Scripture is inspired by God and is useful to teach us what is true and to make us realise what is wrong in our lives. It corrects us when we*

are wrong and teaches us to do what is right. God uses it to prepare and equip his people to do every good work.

We have been programmed to think that 'more is always better'. All of which led Oliver James to talk about a 'disease' he identified by the name 'Affluenza'. Commenting on his thesis, Andrew J. Oswald, Professor of Economics at Warwick, has said: "Mental well-being is worsening through time. The reason is the virus of materialism."[1]

We instinctively feel that 'two is always preferable to one'. But when we are tempted to think like this, it might help to remember some words attributed to J. D. Rockefeller, founder of the Standard Oil Company. When asked how much money we need to make a man happy, he is said to have replied, "Just a little bit more".

Indeed, the memory verse above, which comes from the book of Ecclesiastes, would go further since it suggests that there are times when it might be better to have less rather than more.

Watch Video 3
Ownership and Possessions – Less is More

As we continue with this study, it would be helpful for you to honestly evaluate what you consider to be really important. Answer this question: If you knew you only had a limited time to live, what you put on your 'bucket list'?

Additionally, imagine you have been given a bag of minutes (a bag full of TIME). Time, after all, is probably our most precious asset. How would you spend this time? We can readily identify what matters to us by reflecting on how we use our time.

The author of Psalm 119 obviously understood the need to have sensible priorities, which is why he said:

Turn my heart toward your statutes and not toward selfish gain.

Turn my eyes away from worthless things; preserve my life according to your word.

Fulfil your promise to your servant, so that you may be feared.
Psalm 119:36-38.

---

1   Affluenza: A Review, Andrew Oswald, Professor of Economics and ESRC Professorial Fellow, Department of Economics, University of Warwick, Email: andrew.oswald@warwick.ac.uk

The New Living Translation captures these sentiments beautifully:

Give me an eagerness for your laws rather than a love for money!

Turn my eyes from worthless things, and give me life through your word.

Reassure me of your promise, made to those who fear you.

And this makes sense if you accept the premise that, in the beginning, God created the heavens and the earth. For if He created them, then they belong to Him. The psalmists assert this very clearly. Take these three examples:

The earth is the Lord's, and everything in it.
Psalm 24:1.

for every animal of the forest is mine, and the cattle on a thousand hills.
Psalm 50:10.

'The silver is mine and the gold is mine,' declares the Lord Almighty.
Haggai 2:8.

If this is true, we are wrong to think of things as 'ours'. We have been created in His image and are supposed to serve as 'living reminders' that everything in this world belongs to Him; we have them 'on trust' with the responsibility to use them in a way that pleases Him.

Then God said, "Let us make mankind in our image, in our likeness, so that they may rule over the fish in the sea and the birds in the sky, over the livestock and all the wild animals, and over all the creatures that move along the ground."

So God created mankind in his own image, in the image of God he created them; male and female he created them.

God blessed them and said to them, "Be fruitful and increase in number; fill the earth and subdue it. Rule over the fish in the sea and the birds in the sky and over every living creature that moves on the ground."
Genesis 1:26-28.

We see this reflected in yet another Psalm:

You made them rulers over the works of your hands; you put everything under their feet.
Psalm 8:6.

The New Testament uses the very helpful image of the 'oikomenos' (steward). In Jesus' day, the 'oikomenos' managed the household affairs. The householder entrusted him with the care of his receipts and his expenditure, as well as the duty of ensuring that every other member of the household was given his or her due.

 Watch Video 5
What is Stewardship? – Less is More

Jesus obviously saw things this way, as we can see from this passage in Luke's Gospel where He warned His disciples:

"So if you have not been trustworthy in handling worldly wealth, who will trust you with true riches?"
Luke 16:11.

And He continues:

"No servant can serve two masters. Either you will hate the one and love the other, or you will be devoted to the one and despise the other. You cannot serve both God and money."
Luke 16:13.

Put simply, we must make a choice. When 'push comes to shove' we cannot have it both ways. We can let God rule our hearts and lives or we can allow created things to take His place (and that is nothing short of idolatry). Serving both is not an option.

Moreover, Jesus would have us know that the way we manage the 'little things' (money, for example) reveals whether God can trust us with His 'true riches'. That's a sobering thought. If we can't use our possessions properly, it's a sign that God can't trust us with the things that He really thinks are important. Seen this way, our possessions are a test of our reliability.

But we need to put things in perspective. God wants our hearts, not our money; for when He has our hearts, the rest will follow.

 **PAUSE FOR THOUGHT**
"A Time to Reflect"

To help you do this most effectively, go back and re-read, 'Pause for Thought, A Time to Reflect' (page 9). This is a new lifelong habit, so take the time to re-read and reflect. Remember, you are looking for God's help. He can and will give you a new way of seeing things, as well as the strength you need to develop new patterns of behaviour when you ask Him.

God is the Creator and the owner of all things

The earth is the Lord's, and everything in it, the world, and all who live in it.
Psalm 24:1.

God has given us the ability to produce wealth

When you have eaten and are satisfied, praise the Lord your God for the good land he has given you. Be careful that you do not forget the Lord your God, failing to observe his commands, his laws and his decrees that I am giving you this day. Otherwise, when you eat and are satisfied, when you build fine houses and settle down, and when your herds and flocks grow large and your silver and gold increase and all you have is multiplied, then your heart will become proud and you will forget the Lord your God, who brought you out of Egypt, out of the land of slavery. He led you through the vast and dreadful wilderness, that thirsty and waterless land, with its venomous snakes and scorpions. He brought you water out of hard rock. He gave you manna to eat in the wilderness, something your ancestors had never known, to humble and test you so that in the end it might go well with you. **You may say to yourself, "My power and the strength of my hands have produced this wealth for me." But remember the Lord your God, for it is he who gives you the ability to produce wealth, and so confirms his covenant, which he swore to your ancestors, as it is today.**

If you ever forget the Lord your God and follow other gods and worship and bow down to them, I testify against you today that you will surely be destroyed. Like the nations the Lord destroyed before you, so you will be destroyed for not obeying the Lord your God.
Deuteronomy 8:10-20, emphasis added.

Money reveals our priorities

Jesus sat down opposite the place where the offerings were put and watched the crowd putting their money into the temple treasury. Many rich people threw in large amounts.

But a poor widow came and put in two very small copper coins, worth only a few cents.

Calling his disciples to him, Jesus said, "Truly I tell you, this poor widow has put more into the treasury than all the others. They all gave out of their wealth; but she, out of her poverty, put in everything—all she had to live on."
Mark 12:41-44.

Money has a God-given purpose

In reply, Jesus said: "A man was going down from Jerusalem to Jericho, when he was attacked by robbers. They stripped him of his clothes, beat him and went away, leaving him half dead. A priest happened to be going down the same road, and when he saw the man, he passed by on the other side. So too, a Levite, when he came to the place and saw him, passed by on the other side. But a Samaritan, as he travelled, came where the man was; and when he saw him, he took pity on him. He went to him and bandaged his wounds, pouring on oil and wine. Then he put the man on his own donkey, brought him to an inn and took care of him. The next day he took out two denarii and gave them to the innkeeper. 'Look after him,' he said, 'and when I return, I will reimburse you for any extra expense you may have.'

Which of these three do you think was a neighbour to the man who fell into the hands of robbers?"

The expert in the law replied, "The one who had mercy on him."

Jesus told him, "Go and do likewise."
Luke 10:30-37.

"I tell you, use worldly wealth to gain friends for yourselves, so that when it is gone, you will be welcomed into eternal dwellings."
Luke 16:9.

A generous heart blesses God's heart too

While he was in Bethany, reclining at the table in the home of Simon the Leper, a woman came with an alabaster jar of very expensive perfume, made of pure nard. She broke the jar and poured the perfume on his head.

Some of those present were saying indignantly to one another, "Why this waste of perfume? It could have been sold for more than a year's wages and the money given to the poor." And they rebuked her harshly.

"Leave her alone," said Jesus. "Why are you bothering her? She has done a beautiful thing to me. The poor you will always have with you, and you can help them any time you want. But you will not always have me. She did what she could. She poured perfume on my body beforehand to prepare for my burial. Truly I tell you, wherever the gospel is preached throughout the world, what she has done will also be told, in memory of her."
Mark 14:3-9.

God is not limited by our meager resources

After this, Jesus crossed over to the far side of the Sea of Galilee, also known as the Sea of Tiberias. A huge crowd kept following him wherever he went, because they saw his miraculous signs as he healed the sick. Then Jesus climbed a hill and sat down with his disciples around him. (It was nearly time for the Jewish Passover celebration.) Jesus soon saw a huge crowd of people coming to look for him. Turning to Philip, he asked, "Where can we buy bread to feed all these people?" He was testing Philip, for he already knew what he was going to do.

Philip replied, "Even if we worked for months, we wouldn't have enough money to feed them!"

Then Andrew, Simon Peter's brother, spoke up. "There's a young boy here with five barley loaves and two fish. But what good is that with this huge crowd?"

"Tell everyone to sit down," Jesus said. So they all sat down on the grassy slopes. (The men alone numbered about 5,000.) Then Jesus took the loaves, gave thanks to God, and distributed them to the people. Afterward he did the same with the fish. And they all ate as much as they wanted. After everyone was full, Jesus told his disciples, "Now gather the leftovers, so that nothing is wasted." So they picked up the pieces and filled twelve baskets with scraps left by the people who had eaten from the five barley loaves.
John 6:1-13, NLT.

ENCOUNTERS
OPPORTUNITIES FOR MAKING THE CHANGE

These interactive small group sessions will enable you to explore and discuss each topic from a variety of helpful perspectives. It would be ideal if the group session was allocated a time slot of ninety minutes.

GROUP SESSION

"LESS IS MORE" | A Blueprint for Living

1. PRAYER

This should be a simple prayer asking God to be present, affirming His Word.

Spend a few moments asking the Lord to give you an open mind and a willing heart to see things from His perspective. Ask Him to transform you from within so that you might be able to *test and approve what God's will is – his good, pleasing and perfect will.* Romans 12:2.

For the word of God is alive and active. Sharper than any double-edged sword, it penetrates even to dividing soul and spirit, joints and marrow; it judges the thoughts and attitudes of the heart.
Hebrews 4:12.

2. TEACHING

What did you think as you read, 'Preparation: Laying Foundations – Less is More'? Did you sense God was saying anything to you? Did it affect your feelings in any way? Has it changed the way you think? Do you think you need to make any changes to your lifestyle?

Watch Video 1
Bought

3. APPLICATION

Discuss the following questions:

1. What does money mean to you? What does it do for you?
2. What do you think of when you hear the following words: 'Save', 'Spend', 'Borrow', 'Lend', 'Tithe', 'Buy'?
3. In what ways do we misuse the money we have?
4. Have you ever considered money to be a cancer? Is it an appropriate word to use?
5. Have you ever thought of money as being addictive?
6. How does money affect your life?
7. Is it helpful to say that money can 'own' us? Do you have any experience of this?
8. How do you view your money?
9. · In the ancient world, slaves could be bought and sold like a piece of meat. The Apostle Paul took this image and transformed it by relating it to his status as a Christian. What goes through your mind when you read these words from 1 Corinthians 6:19-20: *You are not your own; you were bought at a price?*

 Watch Video 4
Stewardship of Money – Less is More

Discuss the following scriptural verses and the accompanying comments.

Read: Matthew 6:24.

'Mammon' is the transliteration of an Aramaic word that meant wealth. Put simply, Jesus says if you are trying to compromise, you have already given in to the seductive power of 'mammon'. In what ways is wealth seductive?

Read: Psalm 24:1-2.

If God is our king and provider, how should that affect our finances?

Read: Matthew 19:16-22.

If Jesus looked into your heart, what would He say about your attitude towards the things you say you own?

Read: Luke 21:1-4.

Is it difficult to trust God when you don't have much money?

4. TRANSFORMATION

Review God's Word that we have looked at this week.

It is important that you take practical steps to apply biblical principles to your personal finances. Therefore, go through the two spreadsheets that need to be completed for the next session. You will find these on the website. You will only be sharing what lessons you learned and what application/actions you will take from these spreadsheets; you will not be sharing financial information.

The results we experience will flow directly from the actions we take, which are always the product of our convictions. It is important, then, that you spend time with God reviewing these biblical verses, asking Him to change your thoughts and feelings, for that will enable you to make changes in the way you live.

5. PRAYER

Compose a prayer that reflects your time together. You may choose to pray it silently or voice it for others to hear. But, whichever you do, never forget that God knows what's going on in your heart and that His plans for your life are always for your good.

PREPARATION
LAYING FOUNDATIONS

These preparatory studies will serve as an introduction to help you prepare for your interactive group sessions. The preparation laying foundation sessions will be best completed in two to three individual 30 minute in the week prior to the group session

SESSION 2

"STRESS IS BAD" | Free to Serve Him

KEY MEMORY VERSE

Start children off on the way they should go, and even when they are old they will not turn from it. **The rich rule over the poor, and the borrower is slave to the lender.**
Proverbs 22:6-7, emphasis added.

INTRODUCTION

We all know that financial stress is not good for us. Think about it for a moment. Have you ever heard anyone say, "Ever since I got into debt, my marriage has improved miraculously."? or "Back before we had payments to make, we fought all the time, but we never, ever fight now because we're in debt."?

Can you recall anyone ever saying, "The massively high rate on my credit card has improved my love life."? or "When I go to bed, I praise God for my debts. There was a time when I had none, but thankfully all that is behind me. I have payments to make wherever I go, and I simply love having to pay these high-interest rates."?

Of course not! We tend to say such things as, "I wish we could give more to help people who are in need. We're just not able to do that right now." "I wish that one of us could stay home with the kids, but that's not even close to being an option." "I wish that we didn't have this stress. We're fighting all the time." "I wish we could travel, but we can't even begin to think of doing that."

Experience tells us that financial stress is not good for us.

 Watch Videos 8 & 9
Facing our Debt – Stress is Bad & What is Debt? – Stress is Bad

Sadly, too many people have very little understanding when it comes to the issue of money, simply because they have had little or no real help. Just ponder what life would be like if you were free of financial stress. Imagine breaking something and having the resources to get it fixed immediately. What would it be like to have the cash to buy the things you need without having to calculate the amount of interest you would have to pay if you needed to borrow it? How about having a week off work and realising that your greatest problem would be choosing from a wide range of attractive entertainment options? And wouldn't it be wonderful to have the resources to help others in a way that you just can't do at the moment?

Here's the good news. You can do more than have a dream. Jesus has assured us that if we are faithful with the little He has given us, then He is quite likely to trust us with more. If we want to discover God's amazing generosity, we must learn to live with integrity.

Here are a few guidelines:

Financial Self-Control

God wants us to exercise self-control. It's a sign of His Spirit at work in us. And so, we are going to learn to say, 'No' for a little while, so that we can say, 'Yes' for the rest of our lives.

Financial Freedom

The Bible tells us that if we lack wisdom we can ask for it and God will give it to us in abundance. And this can prove especially true when it comes to the way we use our resources. For example, it is surely wise to stop buying things we cannot afford, because we all know that there will come a day of reckoning. Why should we be burdened with repayments for goods and services that have long since been used?

Financial Realism

The Bible does not say that debt is sinful, but it's worth noting that every reference it makes to debt is negative and accompanied with warnings as well as encouragements to get out of debt. Such advice stands in stark contrast to the way 'man's economy' works.

So, what can we say about debt? Spend a little time pondering these observations.

Watch Video 10
Getting out of Debt? – Stress is Bad

Credit can be easily accessed and we are constantly being tempted to purchase things we cannot afford. Our experience shows that debt can be addictive, thereby robbing us of our freedom.

Every time we incur a debt we run the risk of denying God an opportunity to show His love by meeting our needs. Viewed this way, our need may well be His way of challenging us to pray.

On the other hand, He may want us to wait until we have saved enough to make a particular purchase (that's assuming, of course, that we really need to make the purchase. I wonder how much 'stuff' we buy but never really use).

Borrowing is very presumptuous. We can be tempted to 'borrow to the hilt', assuming our disposable income will continue unchanged or even improve. But this can prove disastrous. We can lose our job or fall ill, for example, and that can have catastrophic consequences.

God wants to help us when we are in debt. Be encouraged. God wants to relate to us as our Heavenly Father. Rather than condemn, He wants to give us good advice and the strength to deal with the consequences of unwise decisions.

Watch Video 11
Borrowing Wisely – Stress is Bad

'Downsizing' debt can be a long, slow process. Like losing weight, it can take time and effort, resolve and perseverance. Learning to say, 'No' can prove difficult, but we must never forget that the benefits will increasingly come as we seek the Lord and the way He wants us to live.

We can learn to be content through prayer, especially prayers of thanks for the blessings we already enjoy.

To summarise:

If we want to make sustainable progress financially, then we need the ability to improve and address three aspects of our lives and thinking:

- Our practical approach
- Our spiritual view of money
- Our emotional attachment to money and possessions

PAUSE FOR THOUGHT
"A Time to Reflect"

To help you do this most effectively, go back and re-read, 'Pause for Thought, A Time to Reflect' (page 9). This is a new lifelong habit, so take the time to re-read and reflect. Remember, you are looking for God's help. He can and will give you a new way of seeing things, as well as the strength you need to develop new patterns of behaviour when you ask Him.

Money is a major competitor for our devotions and it seeks to divert us away from God

"No one can serve two masters. Either you will hate the one and love the other, or you will be devoted to the one and despise the other. You cannot serve both God and money."
Matthew 6:24.

Debt can rob us of our future

Start children off on the way they should go, and even when they are old they will not turn from it. The rich rule over the poor, and the borrower is slave to the lender.
Proverbs 22:6-7.

God is our ultimate provider

The wife of a man from the company of the prophets cried out to Elisha, "Your servant my husband is dead, and you know that he revered the Lord. But now his creditor is coming to take my two boys as his slaves."

Elisha replied to her, "How can I help you? Tell me, what do you have in your house?"

"Your servant has nothing there at all," she said, "except a small jar of olive oil."

Elisha said, "Go around and ask all your neighbours for empty jars. Don't ask for just a few. Then go inside and shut the door behind you and your sons. Pour oil into all the jars, and as each is filled, put it to one side."

She left him and shut the door behind her and her sons. They brought the jars to her and she kept pouring. When all the jars were full, she said to her son, "Bring me another one."

But he replied, "There is not a jar left." Then the oil stopped flowing.

She went and told the man of God, and he said, "Go, sell the oil and pay your debts. You and your sons can live on what is left."
2 Kings 4:1-7.

God can give us self-control

Like a city whose walls are broken through is a person who lacks self-control.
Proverbs 25:28.

But the Holy Spirit produces this kind of fruit in our lives: love, joy, peace, patience, kindness, goodness, faithfulness, gentleness, and self-control.
Galatians 5:22-23, NLT.

God can give us understanding

If any of you lacks wisdom, you should ask God, who gives generously to all without finding fault, and it will be given to you.
James 1:5.

God can give us a plan

The plans of the diligent lead to profit as surely as haste leads to poverty.
Proverbs 21:5.

ENCOUNTERS
OPPORTUNITIES FOR MAKING THE CHANGE

These interactive small group sessions will enable you to explore and discuss each topic from a variety of helpful perspectives. It would be ideal if the group session was allocated a time slot of ninety minutes.

GROUP SESSION

"STRESS IS BAD" | Free to Serve Him

1. PRAYER

This should be a simple prayer asking God to be present, affirming His Word.

Spend a few moments asking the Lord to give you an open mind and a willing heart to see things from His perspective. Ask Him to transform you from within so that you might be able *to test and approve what God's will is – his good, pleasing and perfect will.* Romans 12:2.

For the word of God is alive and active. Sharper than any double-edged sword, it penetrates even to dividing soul and spirit, joints and marrow; it judges the thoughts and attitudes of the heart.
Hebrews 4:12.

2. TEACHING

What did you think as you read, 'Preparation: Laying Foundations – Stress is Bad'? Did you sense God was saying anything to you? Did it affect your feelings in any way? Has it changed the way you think? Do you think you need to make any changes to your lifestyle?

Would you like to share what you learned from using the budget calculators found on the website?

Man's economy or God's economy?

Read: 2 Kings 4:1-7.

 Watch Video 7
The Widow and her Oil

3. APPLICATION

We all experience tough times. Some of our problems are the result of our own actions, but many are simply beyond our control. Financial pressures, in particular, are very common, leaving us wondering how, at worst, we might keep afloat or how, at best, we might help others.

People react in different ways:

- Some live in denial – as if doing little or nothing will make the situation better.

- Some grit their teeth and charge forward, confident that they can manage things on their own – as they always have done. They determine to work harder or find another job, for example. Whatever the decision, it will be based on the assumption that they can trust in their own skills and abilities. They see no need to seek wise advice.

- Some give up, thinking that nothing they do will make any positive difference.

- Some ask for help from their families, their friends, or members of their communities.

- Some turn to the Stock Market, believing that if they buy the right stocks or mutual funds and sell at just the right time, money will pour in and things will be fine again. Many others turn to money lenders, unaware of the potential disaster that this could entail.

What lessons can we learn from the biblical story of Elisha and the widow? There are three, at least:

Firstly, God is our Creator and our ultimate provider. He wants us to know that:

- He didn't create us to live independently of Him, but to experience an intimate and dependent relationship with Him. This will entail learning from Him, trusting Him and obeying Him. But, just as wonderfully, it can also mean turning to Him for wisdom and for practical help.

- He cares about our 'daily needs', although our relationship with Him is what He covets the most.
- He is able to do infinitely more than we can ever ask for or even imagine.

The widow recognised her limitations, assessed her problem and turned to someone who could help her because he enjoyed a special relationship with God.

Secondly, God has a particular concern for the needy and He has promised to help everyone who turns to Him in faith. Just as He used Elisha, so He chooses to partner with people today, so that He can offer practical help, guidance, encouragement or a listening ear to those in need.

But this assertion inevitably raises several questions, for example:

- Who could you turn to if you needed God to help you?
- Is there anyone He wants you to help?
- In what ways could He use you to help someone else?
  (Make a list of your skills, experience and spiritual gifts. Discuss these with members of your group to see if you can find an answer to this question)

To achieve this, you might find it helpful to follow Rick Warren's advice and discover your **SHAPE** where:

S represents your spiritual gifts

H represents your heart or passions

A represents your abilities

P represents your personality

E represents your experience[1]

Thirdly, God expects us to help others whatever our current resources. But, once again, the story raises some important issues.

For example, God came to the widow's rescue through Elisha, but she needed to exercise faith too. She and her sons had to spend time and effort borrowing the empty jars. And they must have wondered what Elisha was going to do with them. They might have had to face the bemusement and puzzlement of their neighbours.

---

1 The purpose Driven Life by Rick Warren first published 1997. visit purposedriven.com for additional information.

And all they could say was, "We believe Elisha is one of God's prophets and he has told us to do it."

And she stepped out in faith and did what she was told to do even though she knew she had access to just a little oil. She trusted in the God whom Elisha and her family served.

And the outcome? God didn't just provide enough oil for one or two jars; He filled up every single jar she had collected! And, as a result, she was able to pay off her debts as well as having enough left to keep paying her bills. And who knows? Given the kind of God we read about in the Bible, it might have been the best oil in the neighbourhood, or even in the world. Can you imagine the lines of people queuing up to buy some?

It's obvious that the widow 'did her bit'. So what could that mean for us or for those we are trying to help?

It will probably mean doing some kind of self-assessment that will allow us to recognise our strengths and weaknesses, as well as recognising the consequences of any choices we might make.

And if our problems are financial, it will certainly mean compiling a list of our income and our assets, as well as a breakdown of our liabilities and an evaluation of our spending habits. See the helpful guides on our website.

Watch Video 12
Is Debt a Spiritual thing? – Stress is Bad

Read: Paul's thoughts on life in 2 Corinthians 4:7-18.

Paul was determined that whatever difficulties he encountered (and there were many), he would not lose heart. It's worth noting that in verse 16, *Therefore we do not lose heart,* the Greek he used literally meant to 'to act badly'. He knew what life could throw at him, but he knew what God wanted him to do. And that settled it.

Jesus' thoughts on the things we treasure

Read: Mathew 6:19-24.

- It has been said that the emphasis on trusting God rather than finding security in what we possess is so central that it explains why those with vested interests hated Jesus in the way that they did.

- Materialism can blind us and distort our values. It can capture our hearts too and blind us to the needs of others.

- We ought to treasure time much more than we do, because it is one of our most important assets. Indeed, we can begin to identify the things we value most by examining the way we use our time. Time is limited in two ways. Firstly, we have a limited lifespan; secondly, we can only be in one place at any one moment in time.

- Ask yourself: how are you using your time? What does it tell you about the things you consider important? Are you happy with what it reveals? More importantly, is God happy with what it reveals?

Jesus' thoughts on worry

Read: Matthew 6:25-34.

Jesus does not condemn us for recognising our basic needs. In fact, He shows us that they are so important that God is aware of them and will take care of them. Far from helping us, worry will have a negative effect on our lives. We are invited to put our confidence in God, trusting that if we seek His agenda for our lives, He will provide the wherewithal to pursue it. We can pray for our basic needs, but make His Kingdom our first priority.

Spend some time reflecting on the scriptural verses we have read, asking God to change your thinking where that is appropriate. Let Him change your lifestyle where necessary. In this way, you will discover that your circumstances will change too, all of which will produce the change of heart you are looking for as a disciple of Jesus. Put simply, you will become more and more like Him, which is the essence and purpose of discipleship.

 Watch Video 13
Debt Trap: Can we do this on our own? – Stress is Bad

4. TRANSFORMATION

Review God's Word that we have looked at this week.

It is important that you take practical steps to apply biblical principles to your personal finances. Therefore, go through the two spreadsheets that need to be completed for the next session. You will find these on the website. You will only be sharing what lessons you learned and what application/actions you will take from these spreadsheets; you will not be sharing financial information.

The results we experience will flow directly from the actions we take, which are always the product of our convictions. It is important, then, that you spend time with God reviewing these biblical verses, asking Him to change your thoughts and feelings, for that will enable you to make changes in the way you live.

5. PRAYER

Compose a prayer that reflects your time together. You may choose to pray it silently or voice it for others to hear. But, whichever you do, never forget that God knows what's going on in your heart and that His plans for your life are always for your good.

PREPARATION
LAYING FOUNDATIONS

These preparatory studies will serve as an introduction to help you prepare for your interactive group sessions. The preparation laying foundation sessions will be best completed in two to three individual 30 minute in the week prior to the group session

SESSION 3

"GIVING IS GOOD" | Growing in Generosity

KEY MEMORY VERSE

In everything I did, I showed you that by this kind of hard work we must help the weak, remembering the words the Lord Jesus himself said: 'It is more blessed to give than to receive.'
Acts 20:35.

INTRODUCTION

The Apostle Paul shows us that he took the words of Jesus seriously. He lived his life on the understanding that 'giving is good'. Now that doesn't mean it is wrong to accept a gift. We all know that other people's kindness can prove a tremendous blessing. But on the divine scale of things, Jesus wants us to understand that God ranks giving more highly than receiving.

And that's because He knows it can prove tremendously enriching to discover that you have made a difference in someone else's life. It can be so encouraging to know that God has used us. Indeed, the Apostle Paul would have us believe that God wants to bless us materially for this very reason. This is how he explained it to his friends in Corinth:

You will be enriched in every way so that you can be generous on every occasion, and through us your generosity will result in thanksgiving to God.
2 Corinthians 9:11.

But all of this raises the questions:

"Why aren't we as generous as we could be?"

"What is it that stops us from giving more often than we do?"

It could be that we are tempted to think that we don't have the resources to give more. We tell ourselves that we'd love to be more generous, but that it's simply impossible given our current financial situation.

When we think like this, it's worth recalling the story of the two young boys who were keen to stress how much they cared for each other.

The first said, "Hey, Tommy! If you had a million marbles would you give me half?"

"Of course I would," he replied.

"But what if you only had two marbles?" Jimmy said.

There was a pause before Tommy replied, "But that's not fair. You know I've only got two marbles."

The real question is this: will we let God tell us what to do with our two marbles and not the hypothetical marbles we hope to have one day?!

Or it might be that we feel our generosity will be abused, that people will take advantage of us. That can often happen, and we can feel bruised by previous encounters. But Jesus knew what it was like to give without receiving thanks. Indeed, on one famous occasion, He lost most of His disciples because He exposed their material mindset:

When they found him on the other side of the lake, they asked him, "Rabbi, when did you get here?"

Jesus answered, "Very truly I tell you, you are looking for me, not because you saw the signs I performed but because you ate the loaves and had your fill. Do not work for food that spoils, but for food that endures to eternal life, which the Son of Man will give you.

For on him God the Father has placed his seal of approval."
John 6:25-27.

Or maybe it is because we live with a 'scarcity mindset' instead of an 'abundant mindset'. Put simply, this means that if we give something away then we will have less to enjoy ourselves. When we think like this, we need to remind ourselves that God ranks giving very highly and that He can, and will, provide for our needs and the needs of others.

If God says, "Giving is good!" then we will do well to work at becoming more generous.

Our attitude to giving

The act of giving is motivated by the heart. In God's economy, our attitude is infinitely more important than the amount we give. In his book, *Life Works and Legacy*, C. S. Lewis suggests that we should see our gifts as some kind of 'start-up loan' because the highest form of charity is to give in such a way that others eventually become independent.

The proper aim of giving is to put the recipient in a state where he no longer needs our gift. Thus, a heavy task is laid upon the giver. We must work toward our own abdication. We must aim at making ourselves superfluous. The hour when we can say, "They need me no longer!" should be our reward.

The amount we give

Watch Videos 17 & 23
Tithing & What is Tithing?

'Stewardship' is the act of managing wisely the resources entrusted to us by another. For Christians, this means understanding and fulfilling their God-given responsibility to manage wisely what belongs to a generous God. 'Generosity' is the willingness to sacrifice for the benefit of others whilst 'giving' is the act of releasing something of value.

Like so many other things in the Christian life, generosity is a process. Growing in financial discipleship is akin to a journey. We are not all at the same place; we all need differing levels of help for different stages in the journey.

Indeed, the medieval Jewish scholar, Moses Maimonides suggested that there are eight levels of charitable acts:

1. Giving 'in sadness', out of pity and reluctant obligation. It's mean-spirited giving.
2. Giving willingly, but not with sufficient generosity to begin to meet the beneficiary's need.
3. Giving, but only after it has been prompted.
4. Giving adequately AND without being asked.
5. Giving a public gift to someone who is unknown.
6. Giving a gift to a known beneficiary. This allows the gift to be more appropriate and tailored.
7. Giving through another person and that person is able, wise and trustworthy enough to ensure the gift is used impeccably.
8. Giving that will result in the beneficiary no longer needing to rely on others.[1]

Can you identify with these? Are there any others that you think he could have included?

Our relationship with money and possessions

 Watch Video 22
A Blessing to Give

All of this will have more than a practical impact. We will be affected emotionally and spiritually too. And we need to address each of these three areas if we are to make the changes God wants of us.

If we simply concentrate on changing our behaviour, without addressing the way we think and feel, we will fail. It is only when we see our inner convictions change that we will be able to sustain a different lifestyle and experience different results.

The fundamental issue is not what we do, but who we are and, more importantly, who we are becoming. We need to ask if we really want to be like Jesus, because if we do we will cultivate a generous heart. What we do is always an expression of what we believe in our hearts. Generous acts flow from a generous heart, whereas meanness springs from a miserly spirit. That is why God is more concerned about our inner being than any outward show.

---

1   Moses ben Maimon [known to English speaking audiences as 'Maimonides' and Hebrew speaking as 'Rambam'] (1138–1204) is one of the greatest Jewish philosophers of the medieval period and is still widely read today. The *Mishneh Torah*, his 14-volume compendium of Jewish law, established him as the leading rabbinic authority of his time.

PAUSE FOR THOUGHT
"A Time to Reflect"

To help you do this most effectively, go back and re-read, 'Pause for Thought, A Time to Reflect' (page 9). This is a new lifelong habit, so take the time to re-read and reflect. Remember, you are looking for God's help. He can and will give you a new way of seeing things, as well as the strength you need to develop new patterns of behaviour when you ask Him.

Authentic generosity: the right motivation

God deserves all we have and all we are because of what He has done for us. We can see this reflected in one of the most challenging passages the Apostle Paul ever wrote. Paul knew how tempting it is to divorce what we believe from what we do. But this would be to misunderstand what God wants for us. We must allow our Christian convictions to shape our everyday life, because that too should be seen as an act of worship.

And so, in the opening verses of Romans chapter 12, Paul urges us to let God's mercy transform our hearts, our minds and our actions (the way we behave).

Therefore, I urge you, brothers and sisters, in view of God's mercy, to offer your bodies as a living sacrifice, holy and pleasing to God—this is your true and proper worship. Do not conform to the pattern of this world, but be transformed by the renewing of your mind. Then you will be able to test and approve what God's will is—his good, pleasing and perfect will.
Romans 12:1-2.

Giving, then, should arise from a sense of thankfulness and be directed by an understanding of God's values and priorities.

Generosity: some characteristics

It has never been easy to motivate Christians to be generous stewards of all God has entrusted to them. The Apostle Paul understood this only too well, as we can see in the letters he wrote to the church in Corinth.

Paul and Barnabas had spent a huge amount of time encouraging the churches they were in contact with to give to their famine relief fund. The Corinthian church had intended to lead the way in generous giving but, as so often happens, their good intentions had not materialised, which is why Paul wrote the things he did in 2 Corinthians chapters 8 and 9. In these two chapters, we see some of the principles that inspired Paul and that he hoped would reinvigorate the church's giving. They are principles that deserve prayerful consideration in our day and age too, because they highlight the kind of generosity that God finds attractive.

Read: 2 Corinthians 8 & 9.

Reflect on the following observations from 2 Corinthians where Paul sets out guidelines and models of Christian stewardship.

2 Corinthians 8:1-2	Generosity is unrelated to income and wealth
2 Corinthians 8:3	Generosity is never forced
2 Corinthians 8:4	Generosity cannot be contained
2 Corinthians 8:5	Generosity begins with God
2 Corinthians 8:7-9	Generosity is tangible evidence of our love for God
2 Corinthians 8:13-15	Generous people meet needs
2 Corinthians 8:19	Generosity honours the Lord
2 Corinthians 9:6-9	Real generosity is expressed cheerfully
2 Corinthians 9:7	Generosity is a personal decision

Generous giving is an act of divine grace

It is only as God blesses and enables that we are able to give in the first place. RGV Tasker sums it up this way when he says the generosity of the Macedonian churches was "a visible expression of the divine grace they had received for it is the Holy Spirit who inspires Christians not only to give spontaneously and even more generously than their means would appear to warrant but to people they had never seen."[2]

Generosity blesses God

If you read Paul's letter to the Philippians, you will see that he was keen to say thank you for yet another gift to help him in his ministry. He was in prison, facing the very real possibility of death, but he was not forgotten. In fact, this latest gift was

---

2   The Second Epistle of Paul to the Corinthians: An Introduction and Commentary (Tyndale New Testament Commentaries) Tasker, R.V.G. Published by Inter-Varsity Press (1983)

yet one more example of their faithful love for him. And so, he thanks them for their 'partnership in the gospel' (see chapter 1). But as he draws to a close, he says something very remarkable about their financial support.

You will find it helpful to spend a little time meditating on the following verse:

I have received from Epaphroditus the gifts you sent. They are a fragrant offering, an acceptable sacrifice, pleasing to God.
Philippians 4:18.

This is an astonishing statement. Paul uses words that were associated with temple worship. The first term, 'fragrant offering' is borrowed from the Old Testament and literally meant 'the odour of a sweet smell'. To fully understand the implications of what he was saying, however, we have to realise that Paul uses the same image when talking about Jesus' sacrifice on the cross (Ephesians 5:2).

Now, that is a remarkable comparison, because he's basically telling his friends that their generosity pleased God in the same way His Son's sacrifice pleased Him!

Paul also describes their gifts as an 'acceptable sacrifice'. He knew that it's not possible to earn salvation, but he wanted his friends to know that there are sacrifices that we can offer. They include 'the sacrifice of generous giving'. And there is always a cost too, because in giving like this we have to forgo something we would like ourselves.

ENCOUNTERS
OPPORTUNITIES FOR MAKING THE CHANGE

These interactive small group sessions will enable you to explore and discuss each topic from a variety of helpful perspectives. It would be ideal if the group session was allocated a time slot of ninety minutes.

GROUP SESSION

"GIVING IS GOOD" | Growing in Generosity

1. PRAYER

This should be a simple prayer asking God to be present, affirming His Word.

Spend a few moments asking the Lord to give you an open mind and a willing heart to see things from His perspective. Ask Him to transform you from within so that you might be able to *test and approve what God's will is – his good, pleasing and perfect will.* Romans 12:2.

For the word of God is alive and active. Sharper than any double-edged sword, it penetrates even to dividing soul and spirit, joints and marrow; it judges the thoughts and attitudes of the heart.
Hebrews 4:12.

2. TEACHING

What did you think as you read, 'Preparation: Laying Foundations – Growing in Generosity'? Did you sense God was saying anything to you? Did it affect your feelings in any way? Has it changed the way you think? Do you think you need to make any changes to your lifestyle?

 Watch Videos 18 & 19
The Widow's Offering & Lessons from Paul

3. APPLICATION

*Don't let the world around you squeeze you into its mould,
but let God re-mould your minds from within.*
Romans 12:1-2, PHILLIPS.

"Thinking is the hardest work there is,
which is probably the reason why so few engage in it."
Henry Ford.

It may be true that actions often speak louder than words, but if we simply try to change our behaviour without having a change of heart, we will ultimately fail. Paul wants us to experience a "fundamental transformation of character and conduct away from the standards of the world and into the image of Christ himself."[1]

The Apostle understood that it is very easy to do what we always have done or simply go along with the crowd. But received wisdom may not be godly wisdom. God's values and priorities are often at odds with the world. Only a renewed mind can test and discern the best way to live.

Priorities

Read: Mark 12:41-44.

The way in which we use our possessions is a very clear indicator of what we believe is important. This poor woman is clearly the genuine article, because she gives sacrificially. It's both encouraging and challenging to note that when we give, Jesus is watching us, approvingly or otherwise.

Purpose

a. Money is intended to do good in God's Kingdom.

Read: Luke 10:30:37.

Money has a huge role to play in leveraging the good we can do in people's lives. The Good Samaritan had the desire to help and also the willingness to use his resources to help effectively. We are called to look for opportunities to leverage our resources to accomplish good deeds.

---

1 Romans 12:1-2 The John Stott Bible Study is taken from The Message of Romans: Christ the Controversialist. The Bible Speaks Today John Stott. Used by permission of Inter-Varsity Press UK, Nottingham

b. Our attachment to money is a 'test' of our desire for Christ.

Read: Luke 18:18-23.

Where are your true riches? What things do you desire to hang on to? The rich young ruler's desire for wealth was stronger than his desire for Christ. He failed the test with disastrous consequences.

Watch Video 15
Rich Young Ruler

c. Stewardship is about the 'heart'

Read: Luke 7:36-50.

There is nothing wrong with supporting worthy Kingdom causes, but TRUE stewardship is an attitude of the heart and not in the action to be undertaken. Jesus commended the woman for her devotion and love, whilst the disciples criticised the woman for not using her wealth to support the poor.

Watch Video 24
Generous Giving: Practical Methods

4. TRANSFORMATION

Review God's Word that we have looked at this week.

It is important that you take practical steps to apply biblical principles to your personal finances. Therefore, go through the two spreadsheets that need to be completed for the next session. You will find these on the website. You will only be sharing what lessons you learned and what application/actions you will take from these spreadsheets; you will not be sharing financial information.

The results we experience will flow directly from the actions we take, which are always the product of our convictions. It is important, then, that you spend time with God reviewing these biblical verses, asking Him to change your thoughts and feelings, for that will enable you to make changes in the way you live.

5. PRAYER

Compose a prayer that reflects your time together. You may choose to pray it silently or voice it for others to hear. But, whichever you do, never forget that God knows what's going on in your heart and that His plans for your life are always for your good.

PREPARATION
LAYING FOUNDATIONS

These preparatory studies will serve as an introduction to help you prepare for your interactive group sessions. The preparation laying foundation sessions will be best completed in two to three individual 30 minute in the week prior to the group session

SESSION 4

"TOMORROW MATTERS" | Changing how we Live Today

KEY MEMORY VERSE

The wise have wealth and luxury, but fools spend whatever they get.
Proverbs 21:20, NLT.

INTRODUCTION

We've been so conditioned to want things immediately that many of us find it difficult to wait. This attitude can affect the way we treat our bodies as well as our relationships, but it is most obvious in the way we handle our finances.

However, if we take the long-term view and accept that 'tomorrow matters', we will appreciate that we may need to change the way we live today. The memory verse above spells this out with timeless wisdom.

The parable of the talents

Jesus regularly used parables, because they challenged His listeners to really question their assumptions. He wanted them to examine their fundamental convictions and, where necessary, adjust their lives accordingly. We can see this in a parable we find in Matthew chapter 25.

Read: Matthew 25:14-30.

Put simply, Jesus wants us to use what we have in His service. In fact, He would prefer us to make mistakes rather than completely 'mess up' by doing nothing at all. For if we simply hoard and not use what we have, we will discover that He considers such behaviour nothing short of 'wicked'.

If tomorrow really matters, we cannot simply 'play safe'. We will have to give an account of our stewardship. But be encouraged: He is not looking for extraordinary behaviour, just faithfulness. This means we need to ask ourselves if we can be trusted.

In the light of this parable, we might ask ourselves how we can generate money that can be used in the Lord's service.

We can use our skills and energies to generate wealth. This parable reminds us that we can make money by putting what we already possess to work.

Watch Video 20
Spending

Making more money

So how can our money make yet more money? There are several ways in which we can do this:

Trim

Regardless of your income level, ask yourself if you could intentionally live below your means. This will allow you to save. Alternatively, examine what you have and ask yourself if there is anything you could sell.

And don't forget the overriding principle: when we REALLY believe that 'tomorrow matters', we will have the motivation to change the way we live today. For in the final analysis there are three ways in which we can change our financial situation:

1. We can spend less
2. We can make more money
3. We can devise a plan on how we can do both

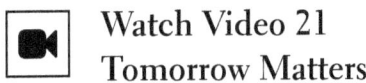 **Watch Video 21
Tomorrow Matters**

Save

There are three principal ways in which we can save, each of which has a very definite purpose:

Short-term savings. We engage in this form of saving so that we might be adequately prepared for any unexpected costs, such as having to replace a household appliance or purchase a new computer.

Medium-term savings. We engage in this form of saving in the light of any expenses we anticipate over the next three to six months.

Savings such as these will help us cover emergencies and unexpected interruptions to our regular source of income through the loss of employment or illness, for example.

Long-term savings. These savings help us plan for the long term. Retirement is an obvious reason for such savings.

Invest

Here are some broad biblical principles that we ought to adopt when investing the money we currently have:

1. **Investment Principle 1**
   Never, ever invest in things you don't understand.
   See Romans 14:5.

2. **Investment Principle 2**
   Don't put all your eggs in one basket.
   See Ecclesiastes 11:2.

3. **Investment Principle 3**
   Don't try to get rich too quickly.
   See 1 Timothy 6:9-10.

PAUSE FOR THOUGHT
"A Time to Reflect"

To help you do this most effectively, go back and re-read, 'Pause for Thought, A Time to Reflect' (page 9). This is a new lifelong habit, so take the time to re-read and reflect. Remember, you are looking for God's help. He can and will give you a new way of seeing things, as well as the strength you need to develop new patterns of behaviour when you ask Him.

Be content and be thankful for what you have

Not that I was ever in need, for I have learned how to be content with whatever I have. I know how to live on almost nothing or with everything. I have learned the secret of living in every situation, whether it is with a full stomach or empty, with plenty or little. For I can do everything through Christ, who gives me strength.
Philippians 4:11-13, NLT.

Don't try to get rich quick

Wealth from get-rich-quick schemes quickly disappears; wealth from hard work grows over time.
Proverbs 13:11, NLT.

Save regularly, set goals and make a plan

Good planning and hard work lead to prosperity, but hasty shortcuts lead to poverty.
Proverbs 21:5, NLT.

Saving for the right motive

But people who long to be rich fall into temptation and are trapped by many foolish and harmful desires that plunge them into ruin and destruction. For the love of money is the root of all kinds of evil. And some people, craving money, have wandered from the true faith and pierced themselves with many sorrows.
1 Timothy 6:9-10, NLT.

The way we use our money is an outside indicator of an inside spiritual state

"For where your treasure is, there your heart will be also."
Matthew 6:21.

The measure by which God entrusts to us His true riches will be determined by the way we handle money now

"Whoever can be trusted with very little can also be trusted with much, and whoever is dishonest with very little will also be dishonest with much. So if you have not been trustworthy in handling worldly wealth, who will trust you with true riches? And if you have not been trustworthy with someone else's property, who will give you property of your own?"
Luke 16:10-12.

ENCOUNTERS
OPPORTUNITIES FOR MAKING THE CHANGE

These interactive small group sessions will enable you to explore and discuss each topic from a variety of helpful perspectives. It would be ideal if the group session was allocated a time slot of ninety minutes.

GROUP SESSION

"TOMORROW MATTERS" | Changing how we Live Today

1. PRAYER

This should be a simple prayer asking God to be present, affirming His Word.

Spend a few moments asking the Lord to give you an open mind and a willing heart to see things from His perspective. Ask Him to transform you from within so that you might be able to *test and approve what God's will is – his good, pleasing and perfect will.* Romans 12:2.

For the word of God is alive and active. Sharper than any double-edged sword, it penetrates even to dividing soul and spirit, joints and marrow; it judges the thoughts and attitudes of the heart.
Hebrews 4:12.

2. TEACHING

What did you think as you read, 'Preparation: Laying Foundations – Tomorrow Matters'? Did you sense God was saying anything to you? Did it affect your feelings in any way? Has it changed the way you think? Do you think you need to make any changes to your lifestyle?

 Watch Video 6
The Parable of the Talents

3. APPLICATION

What does the Bible say about people who save money? How does it compare to the world's view of using money?

A startling testimony

Read: Philippians 4:11-19.

Paul's letters show us that his life as an apostle was clearly 'no bed of roses'. Indeed, few, if any, of us will ever suffer as he did. He was imprisoned, beaten and left for dead after a mob tried to stone him. He almost died at sea, was severely threatened by his enemies, was exposed to the elements, went hungry and thirsty, and suffered exposure to the cold. In other words, his life was 'no bed of roses'.

Read and ponder: 1 Corinthians 4:9-13.

We catch a glimpse of Paul's inner feelings in a letter he wrote to the church in Corinth, where he says: *for we who are alive are always consigned to death for Jesus' sake, so that the life of Jesus may also be revealed in our mortal bodies.* 2 Corinthians 4:11, BSB. We might paraphrase his sentiments this way: "It's killing me to keep you going."

Given all this, it is clear that he is saying something quite unexpected, if not extraordinary, in Philippians 4:19 when he writes:

And my God will meet all your needs according to the riches of his glory in Christ Jesus.

Questions:

- What is the main promise in this verse?
- Why do you think Paul was able to make this bold statement? (You might find it helpful to read Philippians 4:10ff)
- How can we learn the secret of being content whatever the circumstances? (In what way might it be related to what he says in verse 13?)

A startling challenge

Read: Luke 12:16-21.

This challenging story shows us that Jesus did not chastise the young man for being prosperous or for being careful with his money. He is keen to go to the 'heart of the matter' and expose his real values and his source of security.

It is important to appreciate that Christians can struggle with two mistaken myths about poverty and prosperity.

Firstly, they can overemphasise the place of poverty and asceticism in the Christian life. But such an approach can create a sense of false guilt based on the assumption that poverty always leads to godliness.

This first type of thinking exalts poverty or asceticism, which is severe self-discipline and the avoidance of all forms of indulgence. This is based on the false belief that poverty leads to godliness.

Secondly, it is all too tempting to value ourselves by what we have or do not have. In other words, we can assume that 'we are worth what we are worth'.

God would have us remember that:

- Materialism is simply the love of money and possessions. It's another word for greed or covetousness.
- It is not bad to have wealth; it is bad for wealth to have us.
- He wants us to trust Him, not in our wealth or our own resources.
- He is the source of everything we have or could ever have.
- He can do more through us than we can ever do on our own.

As Jesus says:

"I am the true vine, and my Father is the gardener. He cuts off every branch in me that bears no fruit, while every branch that does bear fruit he prunes so that it will be even more fruitful. You are already clean because of the word I have spoken to you. Remain in me, as I also remain in you. No branch can bear fruit by itself; it must remain in the vine. Neither can you bear fruit unless you remain in me. I am the vine; you are the branches. If you remain in me and I in you, you will bear much fruit; apart from me you can do nothing."
John 15:1-5.

Making changes today

Read: Matthew 25:14-30.

In this parable, the talent stands for a measure of money. We have no control over that, but we can control our level of faithfulness.

GROUP SESSION   "TOMORROW MATTERS" | Changing how we Live Today

The two servants compared
(A study in faithfulness and wickedness)

The wicked servant

Spend a little time thinking about this servant's response. What did he do when he had buried his treasure? Did he work alone or as part of a team? How did he relate to his fellow servants? Did he develop as an individual? What did Jesus say about him when the day of reckoning came? How do you react to the use of the word 'wicked' in verse 26?

The faithful servant

Spend a little time thinking about this servant's approach too. What does faithfulness look like to Jesus? How do you react to His promise that those who are faithful will be blessed with more? Can we learn anything from the following incident in the life of Moses?

Moses answered, "What if they do not believe me or listen to me and say, 'The Lord did not appear to you'?"

Then the Lord said to him, "What is that in your hand?"

"A staff," he replied.

The Lord said, "Throw it on the ground."

Moses threw it on the ground and it became a snake, and he ran from it. Then the Lord said to him, "Reach out your hand and take it by the tail." So Moses reached out and took hold of the snake and it turned back into a staff in his hand. "This," said the Lord, "is so that they may believe that the Lord, the God of their fathers—the God of Abraham, the God of Isaac and the God of Jacob—has appeared to you."
Exodus 4:1-5.

If we really believe that 'Tomorrow Matters', we will make the appropriate changes today.

When we begin to operate on the understanding that 'Less is More', that 'Stress is Bad' and that 'Giving is Good', God will meet us in our faithfulness.

4. TRANSFORMATION

Review God's Word that we have looked at this week.

The results we experience will flow directly from the actions we take, which are always the product of our convictions. It is important, then, that you spend time with God reviewing these biblical verses, asking Him to change your thoughts and feelings, for that will enable you to make changes in the way you live.

5. PRAYER

Compose a prayer that reflects your time together. You may choose to pray it silently or voice it for others to hear. But, whichever you do, never forget that God knows what's going on in your heart and that His plans for your life are always for your good.

CONCLUSION

A personal message from Philip and Rob:

Over these weeks, you have examined the scriptures and learned how they can affect both your 'heart' and the direction of your 'spiritual journey'.

It's our prayer that, as you move on, you will become an amazing 'investor' and, as a result, be enriched in ways that you little imagine possible.

If you are married, we pray that you will invest in your relationship and that the Lord will bless you and your spouse with an ever-growing intimacy.

If you have children, we pray that you will invest in them and discover the wonderful blessings that can flow from that.

We pray that you will invest in your church and realise more and more that we aren't called to 'go to church' but to 'be the church', using our God-given gifts to make a real difference in the world.

And, of course, we pray that you will learn to steward your resources, recognising that 'Less is More', 'Stress is Bad', 'Giving is Good' and 'Tomorrow Matters'. In fact, we long to see the day when you will feel overwhelmed by the blessings God has poured out and is pouring out through you.

Above all, we want you to know that you do not have to 'go it alone'. Life can be tough, but Jesus can give us the joy and the strength, the wisdom and the help we need to live His kind of life.

If you know that already, then take a little time to thank Him for all He has done and has promised to do for you.

CONCLUSION

If He is still a stranger, we would urge you to take a fresh look at Him. He loves you enough to die for you and He wants to be your closest friend. You have nothing to lose and everything to gain. You'd be foolish to decline such an investment opportunity. All you need do is ask His forgiveness and then let Him become the Lord (ruler) of your life.

The rest, as they say, is a 'divine possibility'!

God bless you, both now and in the days to come.

Philip & Rob

We do hope you've enjoyed **Making the Change**. You may want to develop some of the issues a little further, either in your small groups, church group or in your personal life. If so, **Generous Heart** may be able to help.

We provide a wide range of materials and support to help you, which include seminars allowing you to explore these principles further.

A visit to our website will provide details of all our resources and other books, videos and programmes.

It would be good to hear from you

Philip Bishop & Rob James

For further information visit:

www.generousheart.co.uk

www.yourmoneycounts.org.uk

email: philbish1959@gmail.com

APPENDIX 1
Full List of Videos
www.generousheart.co.uk

Name of Video	Video Number	Page No.
Bought	1	21
God Owns Everything – Less is More	2	13
Ownership and Possessions – Less is More	3	14
Stewardship of Money – Less is More	4	22
What is Stewardship? – Less is More	5	16
The Parable of the Talents	6	55
The Widow and her Oil	7	32
Facing our Debt – Stress is Bad	8	26
What is Debt? – Stress is Bad	9	26
Getting out of Debt? – Stress is Bad	10	27
Borrowing Wisely – Stress is Bad	11	27
Is Debt a Spiritual thing? – Stress is Bad	12	34
Debt Trap: Can we do this on our own? Stress is Bad	13	35
Any Questions 1	14	See website
Rich Young Ruler	15	47
Zacchaeus	16	See website
Tithing	17	39
The Widow's Offering	18	45
Lessons from Paul	19	45

Spending	20	50
Tomorrow Matters	21	51
A Blessing to Give?	22	40
What is Tithing?	23	39
Generous Giving: Practical Methods	24	47
Do you use a Spending Plan?	25	See website
Is Spending Ungodly?	26	See website
How can I Reduce my Spending?	27	See website
Am I still Trusting God if I Save?	28	See website
Do you have a Spending Plan?	29	See website
What's the Purpose of Tithing?	30	See website
Is Giving just another Duty?	31	See website
Is it ok for Christians to be Wealthy?	32	See website
Do I have to Give beyond my Tithe?	33	See website
Will Christians always Prosper 1?	34	See website
What can we Learn from the Poor Widow?	35	See website
Does the Bible speak about Money?	36	See website
Will Christians always Prosper 2?	37	See website

APPENDIX 2
Video Information With Questions
www.generousheart.co.uk

Name of Video	Video Number	Page Number	Key Bible Verse	What are the Questions?
Bought	1	21	1 Corinthians 7:23	Spoken word introduction to 'God Owns Everything'.
God Owns Everything - Less is More	2	13	Psalm 24:1	How do you trust God with plenty? Is it easier to focus on what we don't have? Is it unbiblical to want to be in control of your finances? Should you pay into a pension plan? Advice on trusting God with your finances?
Ownership and Possessions – Less is More	3	14	Romans 12;1-2	How do we respond to advertising? How do we respond in a biblical way? Is it wrong to want possessions?
Stewardship of Money – Less is More	4	22	Luke 16: 11	Does having money come with responsibility? Consider the story of the rich young ruler – Matthew 19: 16-22 How do you spend your money? How do you involve God in your spending?
What is Stewardship – Less is More	5	16	Psalm 42:1	What is stewardship?
The Parable of the Talents	6	55	Matthew 25: 14 - 30	How do we respond to this parable?
The Widow and her Oil	7	32	2 Kings 4: 1-7	Spoken word re-telling the Old Testament story of the widow and her oil.

Facing our Debt – Stress is Bad	8	Proverbs 12:25	Why do we find ourselves in debt?
What is Debt? - Stress is Bad	9	Psalm 25:15-18	What is debt?
Getting out of Debt? – Stress is Bad	10	Proverbs 22: 6-7	How do you get out of debt?
Borrowing Wisely – Stress is Bad	11	1 Corinthians 10: 23	How do you borrow wisely? Should you involve God in your debt? What advice do you have for people in debt?
Is Debt a Spiritual thing? -Stress is Bad	12	Psalm 37:21	What is debt? Is it wrong to be in debt?
Debt Trap: Can we do this on our own? Stress is Bad	13	Galatians 5 :1	Are people trapped by debt?
Any Questions 1	14	website	Additional questions asked with responses in 30 seconds
Rich Young Ruler	15	2 Corinthians 9: 6-7	Consider the lessons from the story of the rich young ruler – Matthew 19: 16-22 Why did Jesus' response make the rich young ruler sorrowful? Why did he walk away? Where is your treasure?
Zacchaeus	16	Luke 19: 1-10	Consider the lessons from the story of Zacchaeus
Tithing	17	Acts 20 :35	What is the definition of tithing? Does the tithe always refer to money? What do think about the tithe being the floor rather than the ceiling? Are we living as a generous people? How relevant is the Old Testament on the subject of tithing? How does tithing and giving of money/time release resources into other areas? How does the answer always come back to the heart?

The Widow's Offering	18	45	Mark 12: 42- 44	Consider the lessons from the story of the widow's offering? Jesus sees beyond the person to the heart of the giver? Giving what you have from the heart?
Lessons from Paul	19	45	Philippians 4: 11-13	How did Paul respond to situations of both need and plenty? How do we learn and apply to be content with what we have? Where are you today on this journey? The life of contentment is a daily journey? Who is on the journey with you and who can you encourage?
Spending	20	50	Philippians 4:19	How much does the media affect our spending habits?
Tomorrow Matters	21	51	Proverbs 21:20	How do we spend biblically? Have you ever stopped to consider where your money is going? How do you allocate your expenditure and income? Planning for future purchases can be a liberating experience?
A Blessing to Give?	22	40	Acts 20 :35	Giving is worship? What is the condition of your heart? Money has the propensity of attaching to our hearts? Money is a spiritual force – Mammon
What is Tithing?	23	39	Acts 20 :35	How would you define tithing? Is the principle of giving 10% still relevant? What is the real purpose of tithing? Why do we give to others? Is it realistic to share everything within our church family?

Generous Giving, Practical Methods.	24	47	Acts 20:35	How should we give practically? Giving generously is worship to God. Giving is down to the individual. Reviewing your giving is important. Tithing is not all about money, but what is in your hands. Jesus is watching your heart. Giving from the heart is the key to generous giving.
Do you use a Spending Plan?	25	website	Proverbs 6:6-8	Individual question – do you use a spending plan?
Is Spending Ungodly?	26	website	1 Timothy 4:4-5	Individual question – is spending ungodly?
How can I Reduce my Spending?	27	website	Romans 12:2	Individual question – how can I reduce my spending plan?
Am I still Trusting God if I Save?	28	website	2 Corinthians 8:12	Individual question – am I still trusting God if I save?
Do you have a Spending Plan?	29	website	Proverbs 22:6-7	Individual question – Do you have a spending plan?
What's the Purpose of Tithing?	30	website	Romans 5:5	Individual question - What's the purpose of tithing?
Is Giving just another Duty?	31	website	2 Corinthians 9:7	Individual question - Is giving just another duty?
Is it ok for Christians to be Wealthy?	32	website	2 Corinthians 9:11	Individual question - Is it ok for Christians to be wealthy?
Do I have to give Beyond my Tithe?	33	website	2 Corinthians 9:7	Individual question - Do I have to give beyond my tithe?
Will Christians always Prosper 1?	34	website	2 Corinthians 11:27	Individual question - Will Christians always prosper 1?
What can we Learn from the Poor Widow?	35	website	Philippians 4:18-19	Individual question - What can we learn from the poor widow?
Does the Bible speak about money?	36	website	Luke 16:9	Individual question - Does the Bible speak about money?
Will Christians always Prosper 2?	37	website	Philippians 4:12	Individual question - Will Christians always prosper 2

APPENDIX 3
Other Books

Bought: God's Direction for Spending, Saving, Giving, Investing and Getting Out of Debt

By Mark Lloydbottom

Bought will take you on a biblical adventure to uncover the ingredients of what the Bible has to say about how to manage finances – God's way. Financial systems facilitate the 'I want it now culture' of today's modern society. But this so often leads to problems. Debt. Marriages suffering stress due to financial pressures. Inadequate savings. The addiction to materialism so often suffocates people of their spiritual vitality. The Bible has much to say about God's financial systems; in fact, there are over 2,350 verses that address everything you need to know about managing your money, debt, wealth, and possessions. Discover the profound impact that handling finances has in your relationship with God while providing amazing insights toward a journey to financial freedom.

Navigating Your Finances God's Way: A Workshop to Guide You to Better Manage Your Finances

By Peter J Briscoe and Mark Lloydbottom

This workshop will lead you through principles which can be found in the timeless wisdom of the Bible, which has a lot to say about managing money and possessions. True financial freedom is not dependent on the amount of money you have. A person can be truly financially free with much or with little money! Money will not set you free. Jesus said, "If you continue to apply my words, you will know the truth and the truth will set you free."

Financial freedom is often described as the 21st-century dream. To retire as soon as you can, with as much money as you can; to do as little as you can, for as long as you can! This dream seldom leads to personal significance and satisfaction. We will learn in this workshop that the power of money can be deceptive and disruptive – but also a power for good, if managed well.

Financial freedom can be expressed in two forms... freedom from... and freedom to... Biblical financial freedom will result in freedom from anxiety and worry, from the burden of debt, from the grip of materialism and from destructive habits, such as overspending and greed. Biblical financial freedom will also result in freedom to grow in generosity, invest for the future and develop inner qualities such as patience, peace, self-control, compassion and joy. Our prayer is that the Lord will grant you true biblical financial freedom!

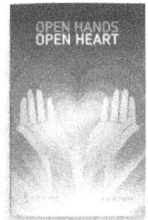

Open Hands Open Heart: Discovering God's Amazing Generosity

By Ifor Williams

Open Hands Open Heart traces a journey of discovery, following two interwoven stories. One is the story of God's abundant, generous grace, from Genesis to Revelation, and how God teaches His people to express their love through giving. The other is the story of a young pastor, his family and church, as step-by-step they discover God's amazing generosity, and learn to let go and give to others. Read, be blessed and learn to bless others.

www.ingramcontent.com/pod-product-compliance
Lightning Source LLC
Chambersburg PA
CBHW081432070526
44586CB00020B/2562